MARVA A. T

M000199850

Time to Thrive

A Busy Woman's Devotional Journal

Keep thriving!

Marva Smith

❖ MatrixSpark

Tortola, British Virgin Islands

Cover design by 100 Covers

Edited by Amy Morgan

Formatted by Tamara Francis

ISBN 978-1-3999-0597-8

Time to Thrive is the guide I've been looking for as I aim to slow down and live from a posture of resting in the Lord while I join him on mission. This book is a valuable tool for any believer who wants to step out of a hurried and exhausting pace, go deeper in faith, and follow God throughout the rhythms of everyday life.

- Stacey Pardoe, author and writer at staceypardoe.com

If you're tired of feeling overwhelmed and pressed down by your overly busy life. If you long to thrive in your God-given abilities by wisely choosing what's most important. You need this book! I loved it and only wish I could have read it years ago. Each devotion will help you seek God's direction and help so you can make wise choices that will help you thrive.

- Deb Wolf, author of *52 Week Devotional Journal for Women*

With thought-provoking questions and timeless biblical truths, Marva Smith captures the essence of thriving in everyday life in her devotional for busy women, Time to Thrive.

- Elisa Pulliam, Founder and Coach at MoreToBe.com

To:

From:

Date:

To my mom, who has shown through her own example what it means to thrive. Mommy, I am forever grateful for the sacrifices you made for us—they were worth it.

Acknowledgements

This journey began several years ago on the last birthday I celebrated with my late father, Edwin A. Titley. The words he lovingly spoke over me continue to fuel my desire to help others thrive.

My mom, M. Joyce Titley, to whom I've dedicated this book, has supported me from the very beginning and, I believe, is still my biggest fan.

I'm thankful for my sisters—those in blood and in spirit—who cheered me on, held up my arms, and encouraged me to keep moving forward. I've also benefitted from the prayers and kindness of family and friends who came alongside and supported me in countless meaningful ways.

To the women who allowed me to speak into their lives, whether in person or online, I hope they know I'm the one who's been blessed.

While writing this book, I was fortunate to have two coaches in my corner. Dr. Saundra Dalton-Smith and C. Ruth Taylor, both accomplished authors, have inspired, advised, and believed I could do this. I'm glad they were right.

Of course, I don't know where I would be without my Smith clan–the JMS collective. My kiddos, Jay and Jan, have been at the heart of my thrive journey, making me a better mom and a better woman. My husband, Sylvester's calm, reassuring presence, has been such a gift. Thanks to his love, support, and encouragement, I have wings to fly, and I am free to thrive.

While words seem insufficient, I am thankful for all who have contributed to my life story and the eventual writing of this book. To you reading it now, I pray it blesses you.

God deserves all the glory. His patience, faithfulness and love have followed me all the days of my life, and it is my honor to praise his name.

Contents

Introduction

Everyone lives, but not everyone thrives. It turns out thriving is a choice. No one will require that you thrive, nor will you be coerced into it. You won't find it in a clause on a job description or as a prerequisite for a course, nor can it be accurately measured in your performance. Yet, it is worth pursuing with everything you have.

Thankfully, it is not as elusive as it sounds. In one of my favorite passages of Scripture, Jesus issues an invitation to life to the full. It is a call to move from merely existing to thriving—living life with purpose and passion. This offer is freely and readily available to all.

> "The thief comes only to steal and kill and destroy; I have come that they may have life, and have it to the full." - John 10:10 NIV

By picking up this book, it suggests that, like me, you've discovered thriving is not an automatic result of following Christ. As a seasoned Christian, for many years I sought to live as a daughter of the King, but privately bowed under the pressure of an overwhelmed and overloaded life. Existing on the surface and struggling to find my way, I was continually sacrificing one area of my life for another.

I thought being driven and determined meant I had to keep moving at full throttle in my career, eager to prove my competence in a male-dominated field. A high school graduate at 15, my country's first female architect, and armed with an Ivy League master's degree, I was comfortable breaking barriers and blazing trails. It probably surprised no one when I became my government's lead advisor in my field of expertise. But instead of delight for having achieved success at the highest level, I sensed something was missing. Resentment crept in as my busy schedule stole time away from what mattered most: my family.

My life had become a classic case of having it all, while no longer being sure of wanting it all. Deep down, what I really wanted was to thrive–to live life with passion and purpose. I kept sensing God had a more meaningful life in store than my busyness allowed me to experience. So, at the age of 42, I made what most considered a rash decision and retired from public service. I willingly stepped away from a well-respected and successful career, which appeared perfect on the outside but was eroding me on the inside. I stepped out in faith, embraced the wild unknown and, with it, an unbridled passion for life and my God-designed purpose. That was nine years ago, and I haven't regretted my decision for one minute.

Since then, I started my management consulting business, created a Christian women's blog, certified as a life breakthrough coach, and mentored women both on- and offline. I discovered a work-life rhythm that works for me and my family and learned through experience what thriving feels like, even with a busy schedule. Most importantly, my relationship with God has flourished even through seasons of deep loss and difficult circumstances. I am more fully alive as I live in step with God's purpose for my life and make choices that align with my God-given values.

My transformation did not happen overnight. It took years of coaching, counseling and a major mindset shift to appreciate what Jesus' offer of life to the full involves. God was patient with me through all of it. This is why I created this devotional journal. I want you to know what I wish I knew years ago when my life was moving at breakneck speed. It is my heart's desire to remind you of Jesus' invitation and encourage you to say yes to his call, in spite of your busyness or overwhelm.

Sister, I know how easy it is to get discouraged, lose steam, and become distracted from the pursuit of abundant living in Christ, even when your intentions are good. So, I will come alongside you and encourage you to take small, incremental steps that will make a difference over time. By touching on the eight core areas of your life, you will leave no area of your life unattended.

Until now, you might have been doing like I was and putting all your energy into one or two priorities at the expense of others. You will find, if you haven't yet, this leads to unbalanced living and an unfulfilling life. Or maybe you're in a comfortable place in your life, but there's still something missing. For help in assessing where you are, I encourage you to take the life assessment at www.marvasmith.com/thrive-challenge/. In just 15 minutes, you will be clear about the areas you need to pay closer attention to as you go through this journal.

Above all, I want you to know that thriving is possible when you remain in Christ. No matter what you've been through, are going through right now, or will experience in the future, you can thrive. Neither your busy schedule, challenging life circumstances, nor lack of direction can thwart God's plans for you.

It is your time to thrive. I pray you will say yes to God's invitation and choose to thrive today.
I am here to cheer you on.

Marva

How to Use This Journal

Your life is a beautiful kaleidoscope of priorities, passions, and pursuits. *Time to Thrive* covers eight common core life areas: spiritual, family, emotional, personal growth, physical, career, social, and financial. (Refer to the index for a list of devotions grouped by core life areas).

To respect your busy schedule, I prepared the devotions to be completed in about 15 minutes, following the pattern:

- **Daily Devotion:** a short devotion on the core life area for that day

- **The 3 R's:**

  o **Read** – a Bible passage related to the day's topic

  o **Respond in prayer** – repeat the prayer I wrote for you or add your own

  o **Reflect** – process your thoughts and make plans to apply what you learned using the journaling prompts

- **Thrive Thought for Today:** hold on to this short, memorable nugget of wisdom to remind you to thrive throughout your day

Weekly Thrive R.E.C.A.P.™

At the end of each week, you'll do a Thrive R.E.C.A.P.™ as you reflect, examine, celebrate, anticipate, and prayerfully plan and prepare for the week ahead.

Going Deeper

If you want to go deeper, I've provided information on additional resources for you.

Who I Am in Christ Affirmations

Knowing who you are in Christ is a key component to thriving, so I have included some affirmations for those days you need a reminder.

Thrive Assessment

To see how you're doing in each of the core life areas, take the assessment at: www.marvasmith.com/thrive-challenge/ This is a great way to establish a baseline so you can see how you're progressing.

THRIVE Purpose Road Map™

Sometimes it's hard to know the steps to take as you seek to live out God's purpose in your life. Use the question prompts in the THRIVE Purpose Road Map™ at the end of the book to determine where you are right now, what you need to focus on and what your next best step will be.

Coaching and Support

You don't have to go it alone. If you sense the Lord calling you to reach out for additional support, I'll be happy to discuss how I can come alongside you. Or share your progress and how this book has helped you so we can celebrate together. Contact me by email at marvatsmith@gmail.com.

It's Time to Thrive

Now, you're ready to jump in and thrive, one day at a time.

Thrive Manifesto

I will show up as the best version of me.

I will embrace grace and extend it to others.

I will take responsibility and take action.

No matter my circumstances,

I will choose to thrive.

Week 1

Spiritual

All In

In this world, we are spoiled for choices. We can pick and choose what we believe, what we do, and whom we serve. If you've made the choice to follow God, it might be tempting to rest on your laurels. But God isn't looking for people who will give just enough to get by or serve him out of obligation. God wants your whole heart. He wants all of you!

Read:

"And you, my son Solomon, acknowledge the God of your father, and serve him with wholehearted devotion and with a willing mind, for the LORD searches every heart and understands every desire and every thought. If you seek him, he will be found by you; but if you forsake him, he will reject you forever." *1 Chronicles 28:9 NIV*

Respond in prayer:

Thank you, God, for the sacrifice your Son made for me on the cross. His all deserves nothing but my best. So today, I offer you all of me: all my heart, all my mind, and all my soul. Let me hold nothing back. Amen

Reflect:

Are you all in? Is there an area of your life you've been holding back from God? If so, write a letter committing to lay it down at Jesus' feet today. How does it feel to surrender fully to God?

_____

_____

_____

_____

_____

_____

_____

_____

Thrive Thought for Today

*Jesus gave his all for me and he deserves
nothing less from me.*

Emotional

Faith over Fear

Faith or fear? Many situations in life come down to these two choices. Take that mountain in your life, for example. Are you looking at the mountain feeling completely overwhelmed and discouraged? Or are you looking at the mountain completely convinced it can be moved? You can't choose both. Fear keeps you stuck; faith moves you forward.

Read:

"So do not fear, for I am with you; do not be dismayed, for I am your God. I will strengthen you and help you; I will uphold you with my righteous right hand."
Isaiah 41:10 NIV

Respond in prayer:

Father, when I am fearful, strengthen me and remind me that you are always with me. Thank you for taking me by the hand and walking beside me during times of uncertainty and the unknown. I know I have no reason to fear when you are with me. Help me to choose faith over fear today. I ask this in Jesus' name, Amen.

Reflect:

How does Isaiah 41:10 encourage you to walk in faith today? How do you feel knowing that God will strengthen and help you when you are fearful? What actions will you take in faith today?

_____

_____

_____

_____

_____

_____

_____

_____

Thrive Thought for Today

Whenever faith is an option, I will choose faith. And faith is always an option.

Social

Better Together

It's no mistake that the phrase "one another" appears more than one hundred times in the Bible, often referring to how we should relate to others. Without a doubt, being in community gives us the opportunity to show God's love in action. What's beautiful is that when we make it our business to love and encourage others, we receive much-needed encouragement in return.

Read:

"And let us consider how we may spur one another on toward love and good deeds, not giving up meeting together, as some are in the habit of doing, but encouraging one another—and all the more as you see the Day approaching." *Hebrews 10:24-25 NIV*

Respond in prayer:

God, thank you for the gift of community and the way you designed us to be better together. Please forgive me for the times I thought I didn't need others and could do life alone Today I ask you to open my eyes to see the community you created for me. Help me to seek out fellowship, encourage others, and be a light for those who are searching for you. Father, I love you and I pray this in Jesus' name, Amen.

Reflect:

What opportunities are available for you to be in community with others? How will you seek them out? Who can you spur on "toward love and good deeds" today?

_____

_____

_____

_____

_____

_____

_____

Thrive Thought for Today

Community is a gift worth cherishing.

Family

Tis the Season

Balance is overrated, so let's get that out of the way. Instead of striving for perfect balance, set your priorities based on godly values and the needs of your current season. Some seasons will require more of you, and some maybe less, but nurturing your family relationships will likely remain at the top of your list. Ask God for wisdom to adjust your priorities as children grow, parents age, and relationships ebb and flow. Let go of the stress of trying to do it all, all at once. Embrace God's grace and enjoy the season you're in.

Read:

"For everything there is a season, a time for every activity under heaven." *Ecclesiastes 3:1 NLT*

Respond in prayer:

Father, please give me the grace to enjoy my current season without looking backward or forward. Help me be truly content and treasure time with my family, knowing that each of them is a gift from you. Let me not be too busy, stressed, or distracted to make time for the ones I love. In Jesus' name I pray, Amen.

Reflect:

How would you describe your current season? How is God inviting you to treasure it? Read Ecclesiastes 3:1-14. What is God whispering to you through this passage of Scripture?

_____

_____

_____

_____

_____

_____

_____

Thrive Thought for Today

Seasons come and go,
and each one is worth treasuring.

Personal Growth

Thrive Wins

When was the last time you celebrated a win? If you can't remember, you've been missing out. Even the simple things and the small wins are worth celebrating. So instead of waiting until you lose all 20 pounds, why not celebrate every two? And rather than wait until you get the new job, pat yourself on the back for landing the interview. Don't just wait for the big wins. Celebrating the little things in life makes it so much sweeter.

Read:

"Glory in his holy name; let the hearts of those who seek the LORD rejoice." *1 Chronicles 16:10 NIV*

Respond in prayer:

Dear Lord, you created us to rejoice in you, and today I celebrate the little wins in my life. Let me never become numb to my blessings or forget where they come from. I want to recognize every small step and each small action that draws me closer to you. Please give me a heart full of gratitude to rejoice in you. In Jesus' name, Amen.

Reflect:

Do you wait for big things to celebrate, or do you celebrate the little moments too? Choose a recent win that you can thank God for. How will you celebrate it? (Hint: Simple celebrations count too.)

_____

_____

_____

_____

_____

_____

_____

_____

Thrive Thought for Today

No blessing is too small to celebrate.

Week 1 Thrive R.E.C.A.P.™

Welcome to your weekly pause. Here you will reflect on your past week and prepare for the week ahead using the five-step Thrive R.E.C.A.P.™ process. R.E.C.A.P. reminds you to reflect, elaborate, celebrate, anticipate, and prayerfully plan and prepare. Allow the prompts to guide you through each of the steps.

Reflect:

How do you feel as you look back on your week?

_____

_____

Elaborate:

Which devotion impacted you most during your time with God this week, and why?

_____

_____

_____

What did you learn about God?

_____

_____

What did you learn about yourself?

_____

_____

_____

Is there anything you wish had gone differently over the past week? What are your takeaways from this?

_____

_____

_____

What were some highlights from your week, and in what ways did you thrive?

_____

_____

_____

_____

_____

_____

_____

Celebrate:

Name three Thrive Wins from your week, including how you saw God work on your behalf.

_____

_____

_____

_____

_____

How and when will you celebrate your wins? Note: No blessing is too small to celebrate, and even something as simple as sharing the good news with a friend counts as a celebration.

_____

_____

_____

Pause and thank God for his love and faithfulness.

Anticipate:

Knowing what you know to be true about God and his plans for you, what can you look forward to next week? Be reminded of who you are in Christ with the affirmations at the end of this book.

_____

_____

Prayerfully Plan and Prepare:

How do you want to feel at the end of the week?

_____

_____

_____

_____

_____

_____

_____

_____

Prayerfully choose three main goals or main priorities considering your commitments for the week. These are your "must-haves"—the things you consider important for you to thrive this week.

_____

_____

_____

_____

_____

Choose three "nice-to-do's" that you can accomplish if you have extra time, energy, or resources.

_____

_____

_____

Now pull out your calendar and plan your week around the things you wrote above, being sure to leave room for grace.

Close out your Thrive R.E.C.A.P.™ time with prayer.

_____

_____

_____

_____

_____

_____

_____

_____

_____

_____

_____

_____

_____

_____

Week 2

Personal Growth

A Fresh Start

Past experiences and mistakes are powerful teachers, but many of us tend to get stuck. The key is to learn from the past—not live in the past—so you can focus on the new thing God is doing. Thankfully, God is not one to hold your past against you; in fact, he offers a fresh start to everyone who turns to him.

Read:

"Forget the former things; do not dwell on the past. See, I am doing a new thing! Now it springs up; do you not perceive it? I am making a way in the wilderness and streams in the wasteland." *Isaiah 43:18-19 NIV*

Respond in prayer:

Dear Lord, I come before you today humbled by your grace, compassion, and love. I am grateful for the fresh start you give me when I turn to you. Help me, Father, to learn from past mistakes and experiences, both mine and others', so that I can move on to becoming more like you daily. Open my eyes to see the new things you are doing and fill me with your hope. In Jesus' name I pray, Amen!

Reflect:

In what area of life do you need a fresh start? Where have you seen God making a new way in places you thought were desolate? How does this verse encourage you today?

_____

_____

_____

_____

_____

_____

_____

Thrive Thought for Today

God is a God of new beginnings and fresh starts.
With him it's never too late to start over.

Financial

All My Needs

God not only knows your needs, but he is also capable and willing to meet them, even before you speak a word. Whether you have a financial need, a physical need, an emotional need, a spiritual need, or a need you're not aware of yet, trust that God will meet every one. While the economy, your employer, or your next business idea might fail you, God never will.

Read:

"And my God will meet all your needs according to the riches of his glory in Christ Jesus." *Philippians 4:19 NIV*

Respond in prayer:

God, today I put my trust in you to meet all my needs, even the ones I have not yet spoken or foreseen. You know exactly what I need, and you are more than capable of providing for me. Jehovah Jireh, I believe that you won't leave me wanting. I give you the glory and thank you in advance for your many blessings in my life. You are worthy of all my praise. In Jesus' name I pray, Amen.

Reflect:

What needs do you have today? Do you trust that God will meet them? Is there a need you have that God can't meet? How does your thinking line up with Philippians 4:19?

_____

_____

_____

_____

_____

_____

_____

_____

Thrive Thought for Today

Today, I choose to fully believe my needs are fully met in Christ Jesus.

Career

Working for God

As a child of God, you have the unique opportunity to shine for Christ in every area of your life, including your vocation. God has placed an army of believers in today's workplaces to carry his love into the world. As a member of that army, you are reminded in Colossians 3:23-24 that your goal is to work with all your heart as if serving God. When you work for the Lord, even your actions and attitudes speak on God's behalf.

Read:

"Work willingly at whatever you do, as though you were working for the Lord rather than for people. Remember that the Lord will give you an inheritance as your reward, and that the Master you are serving is Christ."
Colossians 3:23-24 NLT

Respond in prayer:

Almighty God, thank you for the opportunity to be an example for you. God, help me not to be overwhelmed with that thought but instead to fix my eyes on pleasing you, one day at a time. Let my actions, my attitudes, and my very life speak volumes for you. Give me wisdom to know when you're opening a door of ministry that I may share you more boldly and intentionally. In Jesus' name, I pray. Amen.

Reflect:

Has your mindset been that of working for God or for people? How can focusing on God's reward keep you encouraged and fulfilled in your work? Who can use this encouragement today?

_____

_____

_____

_____

_____

_____

Thrive Thought for Today

I will serve the Lord and do my best to please him, at work, at home, in life.

Spiritual

Come Near

Temptations are all around. Wherever you go, you can find countless situations where sin is right at your door. Don't lose heart, friend. You don't have to fight this battle alone. Submitting to God by acknowledging you can't do this on your own is a great first step. When you resist the devil and draw closer to God, you will be victorious.

Read:

"Submit yourselves, then, to God. Resist the devil, and he will flee from you. Come near to God and he will come near to you. Wash your hands, you sinners, and purify your hearts, you double-minded." *James 4:7-8 NIV*

Respond in prayer:

Dear Lord, what a beautiful reminder that you are always nearby waiting for my call. Forgive me for trying to fight battles on my own. I need you, Father, and I'm grateful that you promise to draw near to me when I draw near to you. You are my rock and my strength. Amen.

Reflect:

What battle have you been trying to fight on your own lately? How can you submit to God today? What would drawing close to him look like?

_____

_____

_____

_____

_____

_____

_____

_____

_____

Thrive Thought for Today

I am never alone. God is always just a prayer away.

Personal Growth

Run Your Best Race

I've never been a big sports fan, yet I was glued to the screen for the Tokyo 2020 Olympics. What impressed me most was how many athletes scored a personal best. Even if their best didn't place them on the winner's podium, they each gave their all—and what a difference that made. In life, you may be tempted to look at what other "runners" are doing, but I encourage you to focus on your personal best and leave the rest to God.

Read:

"Isn't it obvious that all runners on the racetrack keep on running to win, but only one receives the victor's prize? Yet each one of you must run the race to be victorious."
1 Corinthians 9:24 TPT

Respond in prayer:

Father, thank you for Jesus, who ran his race well and left an example for me to follow. Thank you too for the many men and women in the Bible whose lives encourage me today. Even as I learn from their victories and defeats, help me to own my race and run it well. Thank you for your grace over me today. Amen.

Reflect:

Have you been comparing your race to someone else's? Are you prone to beat yourself up when you don't hit the mark you set for yourself or live up to what you think others expect from you? How can you focus on doing your personal best while accepting God's grace today?

_____

_____

_____

_____

_____

_____

_____

Thrive Thought for Today

No matter what happens today, I will do my personal best.

Week 2 Thrive R.E.C.A.P.™

Welcome to your weekly pause. Here you will reflect on your past week and prepare for the week ahead using the five-step Thrive R.E.C.A.P.™ process. R.E.C.A.P. reminds you to reflect, elaborate, celebrate, anticipate, and prayerfully plan and prepare. Allow the prompts to guide you through each of the steps.

Reflect:

How do you feel as you look back on your week?

_____

_____

Elaborate:

Which devotion impacted you most during your time with God this week, and why?

_____

_____

_____

What did you learn about God?

_____

_____

What did you learn about yourself?

_____

_____

Is there anything you wish had gone differently over the past week? What are your takeaways from this?

_____

_____

_____

What were some highlights from your week, and in what ways did you thrive?

_____

_____

_____

_____

_____

_____

_____

Celebrate:

Name three Thrive Wins from your week, including how you saw God work on your behalf.

_____

_____

_____

_____

_____

_____

How and when will you celebrate your wins? Note: No blessing is too small to celebrate, and even something as simple as sharing the good news with a friend counts as a celebration.

_____

_____

_____

Pause and thank God for his love and faithfulness.

Anticipate:

Knowing what you know to be true about God and his plans for you, what can you look forward to next week? Be reminded of who you are in Christ with the affirmations at the end of this book.

_____

_____

Prayerfully Plan and Prepare:

How do you want to feel at the end of the week?

_____

_____

_____

_____

_____

_____

_____

_____

Prayerfully choose three main goals or main priorities considering your commitments for the week. These are your "must-haves"—the things you consider important for you to thrive this week.

_____

_____

_____

_____

_____

_____

Choose three "nice-to-do's" that you can accomplish if you have extra time, energy, or resources.

_____

_____

_____

Now pull out your calendar and plan your week around the things you wrote above, being sure to leave room for grace.

Close out your Thrive R.E.C.A.P.™ time with prayer.

_____

_____

_____

_____

_____

_____

_____

_____

_____

_____

_____

_____

_____

_____

_____

Week 3

Spiritual

You're Invited

The enemy has plans for you and none of them are good. Thankfully, God has a plan too, and his is a welcome contrast to Satan's evil schemes. God sent his very own Son to invite you into a full and abundant life. This is not a humdrum, barely existing kind of life, but one that is full of meaning and purpose—a life in which you thrive. It all starts when you say yes!

Read:

"The thief comes only to steal and kill and destroy; I have come that they may have life, and have it to the full."
John 10:10 NIV

Respond in prayer:

Father, I am so grateful that you are onto the enemy's evil schemes and wicked ways. Thanks to your Son's sacrifice on the cross, Satan no longer has power in my life. I know he has nothing good to offer, no matter how attractive it seems. So today, God, I give you my "yes." May my life show that your sacrifice was worth it. Amen.

Reflect:

How have you responded to Jesus' invitation? Would you describe your life as full and abundant, or does another adjective come to mind? Are there changes you sense God calling you to make to live your very best life?

_____

_____

_____

_____

_____

_____

_____

_____

Thrive Thought for Today

Today, I say yes to my very best life!

Social

When Rest Is Best

For many go-getters, rest is hard to come by. We are often more likely to be found putting out fires, meeting everyone else's needs, and thinking about the next item on a packed agenda. While not everyone struggles with the concept of rest, it's important that we all take time to refill our cups. In the Bible, we see Jesus himself carving out time for rest. If it's good enough for Jesus, it's good enough for you too. So make rest part of your routine. Your mind, body, and soul will thank you.

Read:

"Then, because so many people were coming and going that they did not even have a chance to eat, he said to them, 'Come with me by yourselves to a quiet place and get some rest.' So they went away by themselves in a boat to a solitary place." *Mark 6:31-32 NIV*

Respond in prayer:

Father God, you set the rhythm of rest from the very beginning. As your Son, Jesus followed your example, and

I want to do the same. Father, you don't need my help to keep the world spinning, so encourage me listen to my body, watch for the signs, and pay attention to your cues. May I model healthy patterns and bring you glory as I slow down and rest. Thank you for being concerned about every area of my life. In Jesus' name, Amen.

Reflect:

How are you doing with making rest part of your daily routine? Apart from sleep, how do you prioritize rest? What can you do differently or more intentionally to incorporate rest into your day today?

_____

_____

_____

_____

_____

Thrive Thought for Today

More rest, less stress.

Emotional

Step Out in Faith

God is calling you to do something, and for one reason or another you're second-guessing it. You're wondering if it's the right time, if you have what it takes, or maybe what others will think. This is your invitation to trust God and take the first step in faith and obedience.

Read:

"And God is able to bless you abundantly, so that in all things at all times, having all that you need, you will abound in every good work." *2 Corinthians 9:8 NIV*

Respond in prayer:

Father, you are faithful in all that you do. I confess that sometimes I doubt you and second guess your plans. I even question whether you chose the right person. Please forgive me for my lack of faith. Give me the confidence to step forward, trusting that you will give me all I need and that I will abound in every good work. Amen.

Reflect:

What has God put on your heart that you've held back from doing? What is one small step you can take today in obedience?

_____

_____

_____

_____

_____

_____

_____

_____

Thrive Thought for Today

If God has called me to it, he will see me through it.

Social

Blessed to be a Blessing

When someone mentions the word "evangelism," what comes to mind for many is sharing the Good News straight from the pulpit or an occasional gospel outreach program. You, however, have a ministry right within your circle of family, friends, and acquaintances. Serving and meeting the needs of those in your life, even in simple ways such as entertaining and practicing hospitality, provides a genuine ministry opportunity. When you have been blessed, you will naturally want to share your blessings with others so that they too may know God.

Read:

"May God be gracious to us and bless us and make his face shine on us—so that your ways may be known on earth, your salvation among all nations." *Psalm 67:1-2 NIV*

Respond in prayer:

Father, you are the ultimate giver of good gifts, and I want to be more like you. Give me a heart that eagerly shares you with others. Remind me that you're not looking for fancy feasts or elaborate words—whatever I have can be used for your glory. Let me bless others as you have blessed me. In Jesus' name, Amen.

Reflect:

Have you been holding back from generously sharing God? Do you see how God wants you to use what you have as a ministry to make his name known? What are some creative ways in which you can bless others with what God has given you?

_____

_____

_____

_____

_____

_____

Thrive Thought for Today

I will give graciously because God has graciously given to me.

Emotional

You Are Not Alone

Regardless of how hard you try, there will always be something you struggle with. Knowing that Jesus can relate not only gives you confidence to approach God's throne without condemnation, but it also reminds you that you're not alone. Jesus understands your every struggle, and his Father eagerly offers grace when you turn to him.

Read:

"For we do not have a high priest who is unable to empathize with our weaknesses, but we have one who has been tempted in every way, just as we are—yet he did not sin. Let us then approach God's throne of grace with confidence, so that we may receive mercy and find grace to help us in our time of need." *Hebrews 4:15-16 NIV*

Respond in prayer:

Dear Lord, I am so grateful that your Son walked this road before me and can relate to every temptation and struggle that comes my way. Thanks to Jesus, I don't have to feel alone, discouraged, or defeated. I can freely approach your throne and receive mercy and grace. Oh, what a gift! Amen.

Reflect:

How do you feel knowing that Jesus empathizes with your weaknesses? When you're tempted, are you more likely to turn to God or turn away from God? How can this scripture help you the next time you're tempted to feel alone in your struggles?

_____

_____

_____

_____

_____

_____

Thrive Thought for Today

Jesus understands my every weakness and reminds me

I am not alone.

Week 3 Thrive R.E.C.A.P.™

Welcome to your weekly pause. Here you will reflect on your past week and prepare for the week ahead using the five-step Thrive R.E.C.A.P.™ process. R.E.C.A.P. reminds you to reflect, elaborate, celebrate, anticipate, and prayerfully plan and prepare. Allow the prompts to guide you through each of the steps.

Reflect:

How do you feel as you look back on your week?

_____

_____

Elaborate:

Which devotion impacted you most during your time with God this week, and why?

_____

_____

_____

What did you learn about God?

_____

_____

What did you learn about yourself?

_____

_____

_____

Is there anything you wish had gone differently over the past week? What are your takeaways from this?

_____

_____

_____

What were some highlights from your week, and in what ways did you thrive?

_____

_____

_____

_____

_____

_____

_____

Celebrate:

Name three Thrive Wins from your week, including how you saw God work on your behalf.

_____

_____

_____

_____

_____

_____

How and when will you celebrate your wins? Note: No blessing is too small to celebrate, and even something as simple as sharing the good news with a friend counts as a celebration.

_____

_____

_____

Pause and thank God for his love and faithfulness.

Anticipate:

Knowing what you know to be true about God and his plans for you, what can you look forward to next week? Be reminded of who you are in Christ with the affirmations at the end of this book.

_____

_____

Prayerfully Plan and Prepare:

How do you want to feel at the end of the week?

_____

_____

_____

_____

_____

_____

_____

Prayerfully choose three main goals or main priorities considering your commitments for the week. These are your "must-haves"—the things you consider important for you to thrive this week.

_____

_____

_____

_____

_____

_____

Choose three "nice-to-do's" that you can accomplish if you have extra time, energy, or resources.

_____

_____

_____

Now pull out your calendar and plan your week around the things you wrote above, being sure to leave room for grace.

Close out your Thrive R.E.C.A.P.™ time with prayer.

_____

_____

_____

_____

_____

_____

_____

_____

_____

_____

_____

_____

_____

_____

_____

_____

_____

_____

_____

Week 4

Emotional

Why Worry?

In this life, there are many things that can consume you. You might be worried about your health, job, children, finances, future, or something else that is out of your control. Quite often, we spend a lot of time and energy concerned about things that never come to pass. God has a better way, and that is for you to seek his kingdom and his righteousness without concerning yourself with what comes next. As always, his plan is better.

Read:

"Therefore do not worry about tomorrow, for tomorrow will worry about itself. Each day has enough trouble of its own."
Matthew 6:34 NIV

Respond in prayer:

Jehovah Jireh, thank you for meeting my needs and taking such good care of me. When I am tempted to worry, point me to worship instead. Help me to wait on you in full confidence that your plans are better than mine. You are good and faithful, and I trust you. Amen.

Reflect:

Where have you seen worry show up in your life lately? What are some practical ways you can replace worry with worship and waiting? Make a list of the things you are worried about, then ask God to take care of them.

_____

_____

_____

_____

_____

_____

_____

Thrive Thought for Today

Instead of worrying, I will worship and wait on God.

Family

At Home with Forgiveness

What is it about families that bring out both the best and worst in us? Perhaps it's because we're so close to our loved ones, spend much of our time together, and expect them to know when not to push our buttons. Even within the most well-adjusted families, there are countless opportunities to practice the healing art of forgiveness. As you grow in your relationship with God, may you grow in love and grace toward your family, all to the glory of God.

Read:

"Get rid of all bitterness, rage, anger, harsh words, and slander, as well as all types of evil behavior. Instead, be kind to each other, tenderhearted, forgiving one another, just as God through Christ has forgiven you."
Ephesians 4:31-32 NLT

Respond in prayer:

Loving Father, thank you for the way you modeled forgiveness for me. Lord, I know I don't deserve your love and grace, yet you have lavished me with them from head to toe. Help me do the same with my family. Make me quick to love, quick to forgive, and quick to say I'm sorry. Let my forgiveness start at home so that your name will be praised. In Jesus' name, Amen.

Reflect:

What opportunity has presented itself for you to practice forgiveness at home? Have you been holding back forgiveness from those you think should know better? Is this what Jesus did with you?

_____

_____

_____

_____

_____

_____

Thrive Thought for Today

I don't have far to look to practice forgiveness;

I can start right at home.

Physical

Your Health Is Covered

Your health is one of those areas that can feel like it's completely out of your control. Certainly, each woman will have different health needs over the course of her life, but there is one thing I want you to know: God is concerned about all of you. He wants you to thrive in your health as much as in any other area of your life. Do your part to pursue good health as far it is within your power to do so, and trust God to take care of you. More than anything, know that he wants all of your life to go well.

Read:

"Beloved, I pray that all may go well with you and that you may be in good health, as it goes well with your soul."
3 John 1:2 ESV

Respond in prayer:

Thank you for being concerned about all of me, dear Lord. Your love for me extends to every hair on my head and every single part of my body. There is no part of me that escapes your reach. I know that perfect health is not promised to me, so please help me to be thankful regardless of my health numbers or what any test might say. Let me do my part to treat my body well and take care of my overall wellbeing. I trust you to take care of me, God. Amen.

Reflect:

If you were to have a health goal, what would it involve? What is one small step you can take today to take you closer to that goal? Write a special prayer to God about any health concerns you might have.

_____

_____

_____

_____

_____

_____

Thrive Thought for Today

My health is not immune to God's plan.

Even there, he has good plans for me.

Financial

Generous Giving

If you look around at everyone else, it's easy to think your money is yours to use as you wish. That is true to the extent that God gives you free will in every area of your life, including your finances. However, since you are his child, God is as concerned about your money as he is about your heart. He doesn't need your money, but how you spend it will say a lot about your relationship with him.

Read:

"Good will come to those who are generous and lend freely, who conduct their affairs with justice." *Psalm 112:5 NIV*

Respond in prayer:

Dear Lord, everything I have is yours. Let me not hold back in any area of my life, whether my finances or anything else. Help me to give generously and lend freely from what you have so graciously given me. Give me wisdom to make money decisions that are pleasing to you and will bring you glory. In Jesus' name, Amen.

Reflect:

Are you a free lender and a generous giver? What do you feel God prompting you to do with your finances today? Are there ways in which you can use your money to bring God glory?

_____

_____

_____

_____

_____

_____

_____

_____

_____

Thrive Thought for Today

Nothing in my life is off limits to God, not even my money.

Spiritual

Worship-Ready

The world will make you believe you need to be perfect to approach God. Maybe you think you must present yourself in a certain way or worship in a particular manner. But God is more concerned with what's going on inside than how you look or perform on the outside. He's looking for a broken and humble heart ready to worship him.

Read:

"Going through the motions doesn't please you, a flawless performance is nothing to you. I learned God-worship when my pride was shattered. Heart-shattered lives ready for love don't for a moment escape God's notice."
Psalm 51:16-17 MSG

Respond in prayer:

Almighty and everlasting God, you alone are worthy of my worship. I lift my heart and my hands to you. I know I am unworthy, Father, yet you do not count my sins against me. Thank you for Jesus, who stood in my place so I can kneel before you. Break me, mold me, save me. In Jesus' name, Amen.

Reflect:

Are you worship-ready or is there something you feel you need to do, fix, or become before you can worship God? According to Psalm 51:16-17, what is God looking for? How will you worship God today?

_____

_____

_____

_____

_____

_____

_____

_____

Thrive Thought for Today

God is worthy of my worship.

Week 4 Thrive R.E.C.A.P.™

Welcome to your weekly pause. Here you will reflect on your past week and prepare for the week ahead using the five-step Thrive R.E.C.A.P.™ process. R.E.C.A.P. reminds you to reflect, elaborate, celebrate, anticipate, and prayerfully plan and prepare. Allow the prompts to guide you through each of the steps.

Reflect:

How do you feel as you look back on your week?

_____

_____

Elaborate:

Which devotion impacted you most during your time with God this week, and why?

_____

_____

What did you learn about God?

_____

_____

What did you learn about yourself?

_____

_____

_____

Is there anything you wish had gone differently over the past week? What are your takeaways from this?

_____

_____

_____

What were some highlights from your week, and in what ways did you thrive?

_____

_____

_____

_____

_____

_____

Celebrate:

Name three Thrive Wins from your week, including how you saw God work on your behalf.

_____

_____

_____

_____

_____

_____

How and when will you celebrate your wins? Note: No blessing is too small to celebrate, and even something as simple as sharing the good news with a friend counts as a celebration.

_____

_____

_____

Pause and thank God for his love and faithfulness.

Anticipate:

Knowing what you know to be true about God and his plans for you, what can you look forward to next week? Be reminded of who you are in Christ with the affirmations at the end of this book.

_____

_____

Prayerfully Plan and Prepare:

How do you want to feel at the end of the week?

_____

_____

_____

_____

_____

_____

_____

_____

Prayerfully choose three main goals or main priorities considering your commitments for the week. These are your "must-haves"—the things you consider important for you to thrive this week.

_____

_____

_____

_____

_____

_____

Choose three "nice-to-do's" that you can accomplish if you have extra time, energy, or resources.

_____

_____

_____

Now pull out your calendar and plan your week around the things you wrote above, being sure to leave room for grace.

Close out your Thrive R.E.C.A.P.™ time with prayer.

_____

_____

_____

_____

_____

_____

_____

_____

_____

_____

_____

_____

_____

_____

_____

_____

Week 5

Spiritual

Lavishly Loved

If you have ever struggled with your identity, you are not alone. It is difficult to find your place when the world is busy trying to assign you labels. Look no further. Before you became sister, daughter, friend, mom, wife, employee, or anything else, you were lovingly and lavishly called out by God. You, my dear, are a daughter of the one true King. And in true kingly fashion, he has showered you with his love. So hold your head high, child of God.

Read:

"See what great love the Father has lavished on us, that we should be called children of God! And that is what we are! The reason the world does not know us is that it did not know him." *1 John 3:1 NIV*

Respond in prayer:

My Father, my God, my King, you are the one true God, and it is amazing that you call me your child. God, I am blown away by your love, humbled by your grace, and moved by your mercy. Thank you for making yourself known to me and creating me for a special purpose. Give me the confidence to claim my place in your kingdom and live for you so that others may know you too. Amen.

Reflect:

How does this verse, 1 John 3:1, prepare you for your day? How does it influence the way you live your life? Who can you share this verse with so that they can claim their identity as a child of God?

_____

_____

_____

_____

_____

_____

Thrive Thought for Today

I am a royal and lavishly loved daughter of the King.

Emotional

Strengthened by Struggles

I don't know of many people who like tough times or even welcome them. Yet we read about countless men and women in the Bible who endured difficult situations and came out stronger and wiser for it. Just think of Joseph, Job, and Jesus, for starters. As you read the Bible, allow the overcomer stories of men and women of faith to change the way you view difficulties. Instead of wishing them away, see them as a way to strengthen your faith and draw you closer to our Savior.

Read:

"That is why, for Christ's sake, I delight in weaknesses, in insults, in hardships, in persecutions, in difficulties. For when I am weak, then I am strong." *2 Corinthians 12:10 NIV*

Respond in prayer:

Father, I confess that I'm not a fan of struggles, but I know you have a purpose in all things. Give me a new perspective and help me see your hand at work. Help me trust you to use tough times in my life to mold and shape me to become more like you. You are faithful to do it. Amen.

Reflect:

How do you approach tough times? Is there a tough time in your life right now that's tempting you to give up? How can this verse encourage you to keep going and even welcome the struggle?

_____

_____

_____

_____

_____

_____

Thrive Thought for Today

Struggles serve to strengthen and shape my character.

Physical

God's Temple

As a believer, know that your body is a temple of the Holy Spirit, and as such should be treated with special honor. So it's important to take care of you. Practice self-care, refrain from addictive and immoral behavior, prioritize good nutrition and regular exercise, and get adequate rest. God thinks you're worth it, and guess what? You are.

Read:

"Do you not know that your bodies are temples of the Holy Spirit, who is in you, whom you have received from God? You are not your own; you were bought at a price. Therefore honor God with your bodies." *1 Corinthians 6:19-20 NIV*

Respond in prayer:

Heavenly Father, thank you for loving me so much that you gave your Son for me and put your Holy Spirit to dwell in me. I am humbled by your love and want to honor you in every way. May my love for you be evident in the way I treat my body, with special love and respect. In Jesus' name, Amen.

Reflect:

Do you treat your body with love and respect? If the way you treat your body reflected how you treat God, what would that say? List three things you can do over the next week to honor God with your body.

_____

_____

_____

_____

_____

_____

_____

_____

Thrive Thought for Today

My body is worthy of love, honor, and respect.

Career

Confident Obedience

Even the most accomplished woman will experience feelings of doubt or inadequacy at some point. It's not uncommon to think we're ill-equipped for the responsibilities and even the opportunities we've been given, which often leaves us overwhelmed and anxious. But take heart. God is not calling you to do the impossible, he simply asks for your obedience. You focus on obedience and let God handle the results.

Read:

"Only be strong and very courageous, being careful to do according to all the law that Moses my servant commanded you. Do not turn from it to the right hand or to the left, that you may have good success wherever you go." *Joshua 1:7 ESV*

Respond in prayer:

Father God, when I feel overwhelmed or weak, anxious or afraid, remind me that you are with me. Keep my eyes and my heart focused on your laws that I may be steadfast in my obedience. Strengthen me so that I can walk in your ways and trust you for the outcome. Help me to focus on obedience and leave the results to you. I know that you will never take me where your love can't reach me. Amen.

Reflect:

When are you most tempted to turn away from God's commands? How can this verse help you to be strong and courageous in the face of temptations? Is your definition of success aligned with God's? Do you need to redefine what success means to you?

_____

_____

_____

_____

_____

_____

Thrive Thought for Today

I have nothing to fear. I will focus on obedience and trust God with the results.

Social

Filled to Overflowing

What are you filling up with? If you fill up with anger, fear, bitterness, and frustration, you'll always find yourself in toxic situations. But if you fill up with the things of God, such as love, joy, peace, and patience, your relationships will flourish. Not only will you be personally fulfilled, but everyone around you will reap the rewards.

Read:

"But the fruit of the Spirit is love, joy, peace, forbearance, kindness, goodness, faithfulness, gentleness and self-control. Against such things there is no law." *Galatians 5:22-23 NIV*

Respond in prayer:

Abba, Father, empty me of all that displeases you and pour yourself into me. Fill me so much that your love spills over to those around me, that they may see and know you. Let me long for more of you each day and give you the honor and glory you deserve. I pray this in the wonderful name of your one and only Son, Jesus Christ. Amen.

Reflect:

What have you been filling up with? Will that bring glory to God and point others to him? Choose one quality from Galatians 5:22-23 to fill up with today.

_____

_____

_____

_____

_____

_____

_____

_____

Thrive Thought for Today

Today, I will fill up with all that's good and godly.

Week 5 Thrive R.E.C.A.P.™

Welcome to your weekly pause. Here you will reflect on your past week and prepare for the week ahead using the five-step Thrive R.E.C.A.P.™ process. R.E.C.A.P. reminds you to reflect, elaborate, celebrate, anticipate, and prayerfully plan and prepare. Allow the prompts to guide you through each of the steps.

Reflect:

How do you feel as you look back on your week?

_____

_____

Elaborate:

Which devotion impacted you most during your time with God this week, and why?

_____

_____

_____

What did you learn about God?

_____

_____

What did you learn about yourself?

_____

_____

_____

Is there anything you wish had gone differently over the past week? What are your takeaways from this?

_____

_____

_____

What were some highlights from your week, and in what ways did you thrive?

_____

_____

_____

_____

_____

_____

_____

Celebrate:

Name three Thrive Wins from your week, including how you saw God work on your behalf.

_____

_____

_____

_____

_____

_____

How and when will you celebrate your wins? Note: No blessing is too small to celebrate, and even something as simple as sharing the good news with a friend counts as a celebration.

_____

_____

_____

Pause and thank God for his love and faithfulness.

Anticipate:

Knowing what you know to be true about God and his plans for you, what can you look forward to next week? Be reminded of who you are in Christ with the affirmations at the end of this book.

_____

_____

Prayerfully Plan and Prepare:

How do you want to feel at the end of the week?

_____

_____

_____

_____

_____

_____

_____

Prayerfully choose three main goals or main priorities considering your commitments for the week. These are your "must-haves"—the things you consider important for you to thrive this week.

_____

_____

_____

_____

_____

_____

Choose three "nice-to-do's" that you can accomplish if you have extra time, energy, or resources.

_____

_____

_____

Now pull out your calendar and plan your week around the things you wrote above, being sure to leave room for grace.

Close out your Thrive R.E.C.A.P.™ time with prayer.

_____

_____

_____

_____

_____

_____

_____

_____

_____

_____

_____

_____

_____

_____

_____

Week 6

Emotional

Suit Up

If only the battle between good and evil were just in the movies. Unfortunately, there is a real-life battle aimed at distracting, discouraging, and destroying you. Thankfully, there is good news: you are not without defense. God has prepared a suit of armor that offers you protection and empowers you to confidently stand your ground. No matter what comes your way, you can fight the battle and win.

Read:

"For our struggle is not against flesh and blood, but against the rulers, against the authorities, against the powers of this dark world and against the spiritual forces of evil in the heavenly realms. Therefore put on the full armor of God, so that when the day of evil comes, you may be able to stand your ground, and after you have done everything, to stand."
Ephesians 6:12-13 NIV

Respond in prayer:

Dear Lord, thank you for providing a way to withstand the enemy's schemes. When my battles feel too big, remind me that you are bigger still. On my own I know I can't win, but with you, the victory is sure. Amen.

Reflect:

What are some practical ways you can put on God's armor today? Read Ephesians 6:14-18 for some ideas.

_____

_____

_____

_____

_____

_____

Thrive Thought for Today

I can withstand any battle when God is within me.

Family

For Generations to Come

Perhaps you've received a legacy of faith handed down from one generation to another, or maybe the Christian faith is new to you. Regardless of how you've come to know Jesus, you now have the incredible opportunity to make him known to the next generation. What an honor it is to influence someone else for God through your own walk with him.

Read:

"But if serving the LORD seems undesirable to you, then choose for yourselves this day whom you will serve, whether the gods your ancestors served beyond the Euphrates, or the gods of the Amorites, in whose land you are living. But as for me and my household, we will serve the LORD."
Joshua 24:15 NIV

Respond in prayer:

Abba, Father, today I come before you humbled that you've chosen me to make your name known. I often feel unworthy, incapable, and sometimes even unwilling. Forgive me for shying away from sharing you with others. Show me how to influence the next generation with my words, my actions, and my walk of faith. In Jesus' name, Amen.

Reflect:

How does it make you feel knowing the choices you make today will impact future generations? If this feels like too big a responsibility, what will you do with this burden? Who has God put in your life for you to influence?

_____

_____

_____

_____

_____

_____

Thrive Thought for Today

Serving God today is the legacy I leave for tomorrow.

Career

God-Ambition

Today's work environment can feel like a dog-eat-dog world. Whether you work from home or in a traditional workplace, or you're working on getting your qualifications, you're not exempt from the pressure to get ahead and make a name for yourself. Even if others are driven by selfish ambition, you can opt for God-ambition. One is all about self, the other all about God and putting others first. You get to choose your own path to success. Choose wisely.

Read:

"Do nothing from selfish ambition or conceit, but in humility count others more significant than yourselves. Let each of you look not only to his own interests, but also to the interests of others." *Philippians 2:3-4 ESV*

Respond in prayer:

Father, I want to put you first and consider others more significant than myself. I know this runs contrary to popular opinion, but my goal is to please you and no one else. Search my heart and expose my motives, so that I will put away any selfish ways that are hindering my walk with you. Father, help me to choose your ways above the world's. In Jesus' name, I pray. Amen.

Reflect:

Which do you see showing up in your life more, selfish ambition or God-ambition? Can you think of a situation in which you can consider someone's needs above your own? Look for an opportunity to put this verse into practice today.

Thrive Thought for Today

The road to success is paved with God-ambition—considering God first and others above myself.

Financial

The Source of Real Contentment

Regardless of how good you are at making or managing money, it will always be subject to external circumstances and therefore is not a reliable source of satisfaction. That's why putting your stock in God is a worthwhile investment. While other stocks may go up or down unpredictably, God is the one constant you can depend on. So, regardless of your circumstances, let your contentment come from him.

Read:

"I know what it's like not to have what I need. I also know what it's like to have more than I need. I have learned the secret of being content no matter what happens. I am content whether I am well fed or hungry. I am content whether I have more than enough or not enough." *Philippians 4:12 NIrV*

Respond in prayer:

Father, I am so glad that my contentment comes from you and not from my finances or circumstances. When everything else is unstable and unpredictable, you are my true foundation. Let me put my faith and trust in you always. Amen.

Reflect:

Have you noticed your contentment wavering when your circumstances change? Why is it important to put your faith in God above everything else? How can this passage help you experience peace about your finances?

_____

_____

_____

_____

_____

_____

_____

Thrive Thought for Today

God is the one constant and my source of true contentment.

Personal Growth

A Noble Goal

Jeremiah 29:11 is possibly one of the most quoted Bible passages of our time. After all, who doesn't want a bright and prosperous future? But beyond material blessings or an easy life (none of which God promises), you'll find something even better on offer. Verses 12 and 13 reveal that you will find God and be in relationship with him when you seek him with all your heart. Now, that's something worth pursuing.

Read:

"For I know the plans I have for you," declares the LORD, "plans to prosper you and not to harm you, plans to give you hope and a future. Then you will call on me and come and pray to me, and I will listen to you. You will seek me and find me when you seek me with all your heart."
Jeremiah 29:11-13 NIV

Respond in prayer:

Almighty God, you are never too far away from me, yet sometimes I find myself chasing goals and gods that do not satisfy. I confess that I lose sight of what's truly important, and I ask for your forgiveness. May I never be so busy filling up on good things that I miss what matters most, which is my relationship with you. Thank you for your mercy. Amen.

Reflect:

How does this passage put your relationship with God in perspective? Is seeking God the main thing in your life? Consider some of your current goals. Are they taking you closer to or further away from God?

_____

_____

_____

_____

_____

Thrive Thought for Today

There is no goal as noble as seeking God.

Week 6 Thrive R.E.C.A.P.™

Welcome to your weekly pause. Here you will reflect on your past week and prepare for the week ahead using the five-step Thrive R.E.C.A.P.™ process. R.E.C.A.P. reminds you to reflect, elaborate, celebrate, anticipate, and prayerfully plan and prepare. Allow the prompts to guide you through each of the steps.

Reflect:

How do you feel as you look back on your week?

_____

_____

Elaborate:

Which devotion impacted you most during your time with God this week, and why?

_____

_____

_____

What did you learn about God?

_____

_____

What did you learn about yourself?

_____

_____

_____

Is there anything you wish had gone differently over the past week? What are your takeaways from this?

_____

_____

_____

What were some highlights from your week, and in what ways did you thrive?

_____

_____

_____

_____

_____

Celebrate:

Name three Thrive Wins from your week, including how you saw God work on your behalf.

_____

_____

_____

_____

_____

How and when will you celebrate your wins? Note: No blessing is too small to celebrate, and even something as simple as sharing the good news with a friend counts as a celebration.

_____

_____

_____

Pause and thank God for his love and faithfulness.

Anticipate:

Knowing what you know to be true about God and his plans for you, what can you look forward to next week? Be reminded of who you are in Christ with the affirmations at the end of this book.

_____

_____

Prayerfully Plan and Prepare:

How do you want to feel at the end of the week?

_____

_____

_____

_____

_____

_____

_____

_____

Prayerfully choose three main goals or main priorities considering your commitments for the week. These are your "must-haves"—the things you consider important for you to thrive this week.

_____

_____

_____

_____

_____

_____

Choose three "nice-to-do's" that you can accomplish if you have extra time, energy, or resources.

_____

_____

_____

Now pull out your calendar and plan your week around the things you wrote above, being sure to leave room for grace.

Close out your Thrive R.E.C.A.P.™ time with prayer.

_____

_____

_____

_____

_____

_____

_____

_____

_____

_____

_____

_____

_____

_____

_____

Who I Am in Christ – Affirmations

1. I am a conqueror.

"No, in all these things we are more than conquerors through him who loved us." **Romans 8:37 ESV**

2. I am righteous.

"For our sake he made him to be sin who knew no sin, so that in him we might become the righteousness of God." **2 Corinthians 5:21 ESV**

3. I am a child of God.

"And because you are sons, God has sent the Spirit of his Son into our hearts, crying, 'Abba! Father!' So you are no longer a slave, but a son, and if a son, then an heir through God." **Galatians 4:6-7 ESV**

"For all who are led by the Spirit of God are sons of God. For you did not receive the spirit of slavery to fall back into fear, but you have received the Spirit of adoption as sons, by whom we cry, 'Abba! Father!'" **Romans 8:14-15 ESV**

"But to all who did receive him, who believed in his name, he gave the right to become children of God." **John 1:12 ESV**

4. I am blessed.

"Blessed be the God and Father of our Lord Jesus Christ, who has blessed us in Christ with every spiritual blessing in the heavenly places." **Ephesians 1:3 ESV**

5. I am capable.

"I can do all things through him who strengthens me." **Philippians 4:13 ESV**

6. I am a light.

"You are the light of the world. A city set on a hill cannot be hidden." **Matthew 5:14 ESV**

7. I am called.

"Only let each person lead the life that the Lord has assigned to him, and to which God has called him." **1 Corinthians 7:17 ESV**

8. I am victorious.

"But thanks be to God, who gives us the victory through our Lord Jesus Christ." **1 Corinthians 15:57 ESV**

9. I am blameless.

"He has now reconciled [you] in his body of flesh by his death, in order to present you holy and blameless and above reproach before him." **Colossians 1:22 ESV**

10. I am complete.

"And in Christ you have been brought to fullness." **Colossians 2:10 NIV**

11. I am loved.

"This is love: not that we loved God, but that he loved us and sent his Son as an atoning sacrifice for our sins." **1 John 4:10 NIV**

THRIVE Purpose Road Map™

Follow the THRIVE Purpose Road Map™ to gain clarity following these six steps:

- T – take stock

- H – home in on what's important

- R – reimagine what's possible

- I – identify the obstacles

- V – envision the victory

- E – execute the plan

See the THRIVE Purpose Road Map™ at the end of this section. Now use the following prompts to determine where you are right now, what you need to focus on and what your next best step will be.

T – TAKE STOCK

1. Where are you now in relation to your goals or where you want to be? Start with a THRIVE assessment to answer this first question. Access the assessment at this link: www.marvasmith.com/thrive-challenge/

2.   What's going on in your world?

3.   What's working well and conversely, what isn't?

4.   What do you want?

H – HOME IN ON WHAT'S IMPORTANT

5.   What are your core values?

6.   How are you living your values?

7.   In what areas are you out of sync?

8.   What fills you up?

9.   What drains your energy?

R – REIMAGINE THE POSSIBILITIES

10. What does your dream life look like?

11. What would reaching your goal make possible?

12. How would your life be better?

13. What options and opportunities are available?

14. What is exciting to you about this?

I – IDENTIFY THE OBSTACLES

15. What obstacles are standing in your way (in your mind and in your lifestyle)?

16. What roadblocks do you anticipate?

17. How can you address those roadblocks?

V – ENVISION THE VICTORY

18. What changes do you need to make to win?

19. What resources and support do you need?

20. Who's in your victory circle?

E - EXECUTE THE PLAN

21. What's your next best step?

22. What daily actions do you need to take?

23. How will you know when you're on or off track?

24. When are you going to start?

25. What small change or shift can you make today?

THRIVE *Purpose* Road Map™

Index of Devotions by Core Life Area

Spiritual: All In; Come Near; You're Invited; Worship-Ready; and Lavishly Loved

Family: Tis the Season; At Home with Forgiveness; and For Generations to Come

Emotional: Faith Over Fear; You Are Not Alone; Why Worry; Strengthened by Struggles; and Suit Up

Personal Growth: Thrive Wins; A Fresh Start; Run Your Best Race; Step Out in Faith; and A Noble Goal

Physical: When Rest is Best; Your Health is Covered; and God's Temple

Career: Working for God; Confident Obedience; and God-Ambition

Social: Better Together; Blessed to be a Blessing; and Filled to Overflowing

Financial: All My Needs; Generous Giving; and The Source of Real Contentment

About the Author

MARVA A. TITLEY-SMITH is a Caribbean-based management & leadership consultant, work and life coach, writer, and co-author of *She Writes for Him: Black Voices of Wisdom.* Yet, her favorite titles are daughter of God, wife to her husband of 18 years, and mom to two teens. At 42, she retired from a successful public service career and began an exciting journey of self-rediscovery.

As a Certified Life Breakthrough Coach, Marva is passionate about equipping, inspiring, and empowering women to thrive beyond the nine to five so they can fully live with purpose and passion. She does this through her courses, curated events, individual and group coaching, and her online community: Time to Thrive Women.

She starts her day with her Bible and coffee, while drinking in the picturesque view from her hilltop veranda in the British Virgin Islands. Follow Marva on social media @marvatsmith and on her website, MarvaSmith.com.

Made in the USA
Middletown, DE
05 March 2022

62171851R00083